31 Days for the Kingdom

A Devotional with Global Impact

JEFF BOESEL

Fruit Salad
PUBLISHING

31 Days for the Kingdom

Some of the data used in the *Pray for the Kingdom* section was adapted from Operation World.

Mandryk, Jason, and Patrick J. St. G. Johnstone. 2010. Operation world. Colorado Springs, CO: Biblica Publishing.

Introduction

Thank you for joining me for the next thirty-one days as we focus our hearts on advancing the kingdom of God around the world.

Each day we will consider different topics about making an impact on the people around you, in your community and the rest of the world. Some of the reflections are meant to be convicting, to move us to action and other topics are intended to help us realize that God is the one who is at work and all we need to do is be obedient to him with what we have. Still, other topics are meant to be encouraging and uplifting. All of these different thoughts relate to advancing the kingdom in our "Jerusalem, Judea, Samaria and the uttermost parts of the earth."

Following the reflection of each day are questions to help us go deeper into what the topic means to us personally. You may not be able to put answers down right away, but as you process throughout the day, things may come to you. Fill those in the next day before you begin the new reading.

After the questions section is a guide to prayer, which is the most powerful way we can have an impact on the world around us. We begin the month committing ourselves to God's will and praying for our family, our church, our communities, and our leaders. In the second week, we transition to praying around the world, moving from one major geographic area to the next. Before the end of the month, you will have prayed for the people of every country in the world. Finally, we pray for the three major non-Christian religions as we close out the month.

Each day also has a section for notes. Use this section to jot down what God is saying to you as you reflect on the topic of the day. Use it as a prayer journal. Use it to record commitments you make to God and then share those commitments with someone close to you. Often, things that we write down and share are things upon which we act.

Divine Direction

Sometimes the cloud would settle only overnight, and they would march when the cloud ascended in the morning. Whether it was day or night, they would march when the cloud ascended. Whether it was two days, or a month, or a long time, the Israelites would camp so long as the cloud lingered on the dwelling and settled on it. They wouldn't march. But when it ascended, they would march.

NUMBERS 9:21-22

G etting involved in kingdom work should be an act of obedience to divine direction. God has gifted you and guided you to this point with a purpose: to glorify him with your life. Divine direction, though, is not always easy to understand, because God's line of thinking is usually not in sync with our line of thinking. Many biblical stories illustrate this truth, but for now let's consider the experience of Philip, a short-term missionary sent from Jerusalem by God just as the church was getting its start.

Philip had been active among the believers in Jerusalem, speaking and serving as there was need. He had been selected by the apostles to act as a deacon, ensuring that the needs of the people gathering there were met. Without warning, his colleague Stephen was martyred by the Jewish leaders, and they were making threats against all the leaders of the Way. Philip threw some stuff in his backpack and headed to a place he knew he would not be followed: Samaria. He continued to spread the good news as he went, and God blessed his words and actions. Many Samaritans came to a living faith in Jesus.

One day, an angel appeared to him. Philip had heard of angels visiting other followers of the Way. What could this mean?

"Philip, head to the south and catch the desert road from Jerusalem toward Gaza," the angel instructed. That was it. No more than that—just a direction and a road. Once again Philip shouldered his backpack and headed out, back to Jerusalem and then on toward Gaza.

Not far out of Jerusalem he stopped to rest under the shade of some olive trees. As he rested, a well-outfitted chariot rolled in to rest its horses and its entourage. In the back of the chariot sat the treasurer for the queen of Ethiopia, who had been in Jerusalem to worship and was now on his way home.

"Go and stand next to that chariot," the Spirit instructed. Philip recognized the voice and obeyed immediately. The Ethiopian was reading from the prophet Isaiah.

"Do you understand what you are reading?" Philip asked.

The Ethiopian did not, so Philip started by explaining the words of Isaiah and finished with the story of Jesus. They were on their way by now, and as they passed some water the Ethiopian asked to be baptized.

Philip baptized the man, and then the Spirit transported Philip away. He later appeared in Azotus and preached his way back to his hometown of Caesarea.

We should notice three things in this story related to divine direction:

1. **Divine direction is always clear.**

   Philip heard directly from an angel. That is not as common today, but if God wants you to do something special for him, he will make his will obvious. It will be so obvious that if you don't do it, you will know you are disobeying.

2. **Divine direction does not always take you where you think it will.**

   Philip thought he was on his way to Gaza. He never got there. He also never anticipated what God had in store. The Ethiopian was why he was on that road. Sometimes God needs to get us on the road before he can clearly tell us the final objective. Other times the road leads through suffering as part of God's plan for us at that moment. No matter what the path or the destination, our only responsibility is to obey.

3. **Divine direction always comes with power.**

   In Philip's story it was the power to transport him (think Star Trek) from that spot to Azotus in an instant. In other biblical stories you know it was turning a staff into a snake, or 300 men defeating an army of 300,000. As you respond in obedience to God's clear leading, no matter what the cost or consequences, expect him to show up with power.

When we step forward to follow God's divine direction, we step out of the natural and into the supernatural. There will be risk. There will be sacrifice. There will also be miracles working in us and through us.

Questions for Reflection

1. How are you listening to God? What could you do to hear him better?

_____

_____

_____

2. How does God best communicate to you?

_____

_____

_____

3. How hard has it been to respond in obedience to him? How has obedience changed your life?

_____

_____

_____

Pray for the Kingdom

Pray for God's work in your life, your relationship with him, and the ways he is making you more like Jesus. Ask him to forgive you for your selfishness. Give the Holy Spirit free reign in this day to mold you as he sees fit. Recommit yourself to be on mission for the kingdom today, and the days to follow.

Notes

Ordinary People

> But again Gideon said to him, "With all due respect,
> my Lord, how can I rescue Israel? My clan is the weakest
> in Manasseh, and I'm the youngest in my household."
>
> JUDGES 6:15

*G*od uses ordinary people.

Occasionally there are superstars like Moses and the apostle Paul, but mostly, God uses people just like us. It could be that special people are so full of who they are that there isn't room for who God is to share the same space. If you think about the appointments of both Moses and Paul, God had to completely empty them before he could fill them and use them.

Since Jesus is the perfect, physical revelation of the spiritual God, we should consider the people he chose to take over after he left—the twelve he mentored for over three years—but let's start by considering Jesus himself.

Jesus was born to nobody parents. Remember the reaction of the people of Nazareth when Jesus went there in his early ministry? "Who does this guy think he is? We know his parents. He's nobody special" (see Mark 6:2-4).

Jesus was born in Bethlehem, "only a small village among all the people of Judah" (Micah 5:2 NLT).

Jesus grew up in a nowhere village. His soon-to-be disciple Nathanael remarked, "Can anything good come out of Nazareth?" (John 1:46 ESV).

We know that on the inside Jesus was not just an ordinary guy but also God, so not so ordinary at all! Let's consider some of those whom the King of kings selected to lead his movement once he returned to heaven.

Simon Peter seemed to have leadership potential and certainly had passion, but he couldn't control his tongue and bailed on Jesus when his life was on the line (though most, if not all, of us would have done the same thing).

John and his brother James came from a wealthy family and had connections. Their father owned the fishing business in which they, Peter, and Andrew worked. It was John who followed Jesus when he was arrested and got Peter close by because he had family connections within the Jewish leadership. But James and John were proud and entitled. Their mother even tried to work a deal with Jesus to seat them on his left and right in glory.

Matthew was a tax collector. These guys sold out to the Romans and were generally hated by their own people. Nothing like picking a traitor to be one of your close friends!

The other Simon was a zealot, a political radical, who hoped to overthrow Rome at some point, hopefully sooner than later. Can you imagine trying to keep Simon and Matthew from turning every conversation into an argument?

Jesus picked regular guys to hand the baton to; but those regular guys, empowered by the Holy Spirit, changed the world.

If you are like most of us, you are just an ordinary person, living out an ordinary life, but with hopes and dreams that God may use you for his glory. We are no different from those twelve disciples of Jesus. Yes, they had Jesus with them physically, but we have the Spirit of the living God living inside of us. Our potential to know God is even greater than theirs; and, we have their story to encourage us.

Here is a true statement:

If ordinary people will trust God for extraordinary things, the world will change.

Questions for Reflection

1. Who are you? What is your story?

   _____

   _____

2. Have you used this excuse when you've heard God's direction for you to do something outside your comfort zone?

   _____

   _____

3. What is one thing you can trust God for today that would make a positive difference in someone's life?

   _____

   _____

   _____

Pray for your family today. Start with your immediate family and move outward. If there are family members you don't know well enough to know what to pray for, make a commitment to get to know them better. If there are members of your family who have yet to follow Jesus, pray that God would reveal himself to them in a way that they will understand and respond to. Pray that God will use your family to bring himself glory and expand his kingdom.

Notes

So, What Are You Afraid Of?

*He stopped and shouted to the Israelite troops, "Why have you come
and taken up battle formations? I am the Philistine champion, and you
are Saul's servants. Isn't that right? Select one of your men, and let him come
down against me. If he is able to fight me and kill me, then we will become your
slaves, but if I overcome him and kill him, then you will become our slaves and
you will serve us. I insult Israel's troops today!" The Philistine continued,
"Give me an opponent, and we'll fight!" When Saul and all Israel heard
what the Philistine said, they were distressed and terrified.*

1 SAMUEL 17:8-11

*F*ear is a complicated emotion. In one corner you have fear represented by a demon ("the spirit of fear") that deals in the paralysis of believers; in the other corner you have a God-given emotion that keeps us from doing ill-advised things and limiting, or ending, our opportunity for impact in the kingdom. On one hand, we are plagued by the fear of raising financial support, which keeps us from obedience to God's leading toward cross-cultural ministry; on the other hand, we avoid unfiltered local water because we know its effects on our bodies will cripple us in responding in obedience to that same leading.

So, what are you afraid of? Which side do your driving fears live in? Don't fool yourself. We are all driven by "fear," though we may not call it that. A psychological assessment called the Enneagram helps people identify their driving fear along with the strengths of their personality type.

For this reflection we want to focus on our negative fears, those that keep us from obedience— specifically, obedience to God's leading toward involvement in missions. Here are some examples:

"I know God wants me to be a missionary, but I don't believe he wants me to raise financial support." In my line of work as a mobilizer for kingdom growth, this is the number one challenge I hear from people. Sometimes people add that they don't think it is biblical to raise money. One thing is certain: everyone's path to obedience is unique to them. Not everyone has to raise financial support, and for those who do, there is no consistency as to the amount they will need to raise. If I were to respond with a question, as Jesus often did, I might ask, "Do you believe God is able to provide whatever amount of money you may need?" All of us would reply "yes" to that question; so, what stands in the gap between God asking you to go and God providing for you to go? Fear.

"I know God wants me to be a missionary, but I know he doesn't want me to go as a single missionary." This is difficult, because on the one hand a single person can focus more completely on the task; on the other hand, he or she must do so alone. Facing cross-cultural adjustment and work is often more easily done in community. We know we should not go down the road of placing conditions on our obedience. We can so easily see it in the lives of others, but are often blind to our own conditions we place on God. My response would be, "Are we limiting God's ability to provide a partner for us by obeying him and changing our location?" Once again, all of us would respond, "Of course not!" What is the foundational issue? Fear.

There are many more challenges on the road to missions, like location, language, distance from family, etc.; but as we analyze each one we end up in the same place: *we are afraid that God will require something of us that we are not willing to sacrifice.* As I look at my own hesitations to obedience I hear echoes from the garden: "Did God really say that you shouldn't eat from any tree of the garden? ... You won't die!" (Genesis 3:1, 4). Those first children were afraid that God was holding out on them, that there was something they should, or could, have that he was reserving only for himself.

At the very core, we *doubt God's love for us,* because if we truly understood and believed that he loved us, that belief would leave no room for fear (see 1 John 4:18).

Questions for Reflection

1. What are you afraid of?

_____

_____

2. Is God leading you to do something beyond what you feel you are able to do?

_____

_____

3. What things are you allowing to stand in the way of your openness to that leading?

_____

_____

4. How did people in the Bible overcome their fear?

_____

_____

Pray for the Kingdom

Pray for your pastor and other leaders in your church today. Ask God to give them wisdom to lead well. Pray that God will protect them from the temptations of power and pride. Pray that God will give them the words to say that will bring change in the people they shepherd. Pray that they will be examples in love, just as Jesus loved his followers.

Notes

Relationship and Impact

"If I remain alive, be loyal to me. But if I die, don't ever stop being loyal to my household. Once the Lord has eliminated all of David's enemies from the earth, if Jonathan's name is also eliminated, then the Lord will seek retribution from David!" So Jonathan again made a pledge to David because he loved David as much as himself.

1 SAMUEL 20:14-17

*T*hink of the people who have had a deep impact on your life; people whose influence caused you to change as a person. My guess is that, with a possible exception here and there, all those people had a relationship with you and the deeper the relationship, the deeper the impact.

It's not that God cannot impact you remotely, through speakers at conferences, musicians at a concert, or televangelists. Event impact, though, is often an emotionally driven, first-step type of impact; one that needs to be followed up on by someone who can commit to a longer relationship with you. Paul says in 1 Corinthians 3:6, "I planted, Apollos watered, but God made it grow," and we could go on to say that one weeds and another harvests. Paul's point was that no one worker is more important than another. My point is that all those people invested in someone at phases in their life. Investment requires time. Time invested grows trust. Trust cultivates a life for deep impact.

Another word about impact through deeper relationships: it runs both ways. People in your life will impact you, even as God uses you to impact them. This mutual growth fosters even closer friendships. As a friendship grows, so does the breadth of the impact. Greater trust allows you to share things you would certainly not share with someone you don't know as well, and confrontation requires a faith in your relationship that will weather the possible emotional storm of pain and hurt that follows.

You will experience the deepest impact with someone you love. In love, joys are elevated and hurts are deeper. What your lover says and does will not only impact you; it will change you, or at least cause you to want to work on change. Your willingness to sacrifice for the other's welfare rises above your desire to protect yourself. Consider 1 Corinthians 13:4-8 (CEB).

> Love is patient, love is kind, it isn't jealous, it doesn't brag,
> it isn't arrogant, it isn't rude, it doesn't seek its own advantage,
> it isn't irritable, it doesn't keep a record of complaints, it isn't happy
> with injustice, but it is happy with the truth. Love puts up with
> all things, trusts in all things, hopes for all things,
> endures all things. Love never fails.

Though we often think of this kind of love in a romantic relationship, it is certainly not limited to that. We should be pursuing a loving relationship with all those God places in our lives. We will not attain the same level of love with everyone, because this kind of love is a two-way street; but we should be about moving in that direction with God's help. Jesus died for us while we were still enemies of the kingdom. His commandment to us is that we love each other in that same way!

Who do you run into each day? What steps might you take to grow a deeper relationship with them, a relationship moving toward love? It will take sacrifice on your part.

Nothing of value is achieved without sacrifice.

Are you ready to step up and give up something to love someone else? Let the adventure begin!

Questions for Reflection

1. With whom do you have a deep, loving relationship? What characterizes that relationship?

   _____

   _____

2. What impact would you like to have in the lives of the people around you? What things would you have to sacrifice to grow a relationship deep enough to have that kind of impact?

   _____

   _____

3. Who are you having trouble loving? What changes can you make in yourself to allow for a more loving attitude toward that person?

   _____

   _____

   _____

Pray for the Kingdom

Pray for other leaders in your church today, your elders and deacons and those who give direction to the ministry of the church. Pray that God will give them vision for the direction he wants the church to go and the people he wants the church to impact. Pray for the relationship between the pastor and the other leaders of the church, that it might be an example of the love and respect we should have for each other.

Notes

Facing Down Giants

They started a rumor about the land that they had explored,
telling the Israelites, "The land that we crossed over to explore is a land
that devours its residents. All the people we saw in it are huge men. We saw
there the Nephilim (the descendants of Anak come from the Nephilim). We
saw ourselves as grasshoppers, and that's how we appeared to them."

NUMBERS 13:32-33

*P*art of living in "shalom" is feeling at peace, and feeling at peace often relates to being prepared. We can have victory over many challenges if we are prepared, like when the shepherd David faced down Goliath.

David was *spiritually* prepared. He understood it was more than just a physical battle, and that he was not alone. David's relationship with God was based on a focus on God's Word and the experiences of acting in faith and finding God faithful.

> But David told the Philistine, "You are coming against me with sword, spear, and scimitar, but I come against you in the name of the Lord of heavenly forces, the God of Israel's army, the one you've insulted. Today the Lord will hand you over to me."
> 1 SAMUEL 17:45-46

David was *emotionally* prepared. He knew who he was and how to be at his best. Saul tried to fashion him into a warrior by putting him in armor, but it felt so unnatural, David gave the armor back and went out the same way he would to defend his sheep.

> Then Saul dressed David in his own gear, putting a coat of armor on him and a bronze helmet on his head. David strapped his sword on over the armor, but he couldn't walk around well because he'd never tried it before. "I can't walk in this," David told Saul, "because I've never tried it before." So he took them off. He then grabbed his staff and chose five smooth stones from the streambed. He put them in the pocket of his shepherd's bag and with sling in hand went out to the Philistine.
> VERSES 38-40

David was *physically* prepared. He had been battle tested through his encounters with the enemies of his flock. He was practiced and accurate with his sling. His preparation gave him the confidence to stand against an overpowering enemy.

> "Your servant has kept his father's sheep," David replied to Saul, "and if ever a lion or a bear came and carried off one of the flock, I would go after

it, strike it, and rescue the animal from its mouth. If it turned on me, I would

grab it at its jaw, strike it, and kill it. Your servant has fought both lions

and bears. This uncircumcised Philistine will be just like one of

them because he has insulted the army of the living God."

VERSES 34-36

What giants will you be facing today? "Giants" can be all kinds of things. Maybe you are pursuing a goal like finishing your degree or getting a promotion at work. Perhaps you are trying to overcome some physical challenge, or you have relationships that need to be restored. God may be leading you to consider cross-cultural missions and you are not sure how to begin. Whatever your giants, how are you preparing?

Like David, we should prepare spiritually, emotionally, and physically for the giants in our lives:

> Spiritual preparation – Bring these giants before your God and King. Understand who and whose you are. Rest in God's power. Be still and see the salvation of your Lord (see Exodus 14:13).

> Emotional preparation – Be confident in who God has made you to be. Understand your strengths and weaknesses. Play to your strengths and surround yourself with people who will have your back in areas of weakness.

> Physical preparation – Bring the very best of yourself to every venture. Focus on your health and fitness. Equip your mind with tools that you will need as you move forward. See everything happening now as preparation for what is ahead. Make each moment count for the kingdom.

Face down your giants today. Claim new ground. Fight the fight. Keep the faith. Finish the race.

— Questions for Reflection —

1. What are the giants facing you today?

   _____

   _____

2. What areas of your life and ministry could use more preparation?

   _____

   _____

   _____

3. Who could help you identify and prepare in those areas?

   _____

   _____

   _____

— Pray for the Kingdom —

Pray for the people who serve in your church today. Many of them volunteer their service and do so unnoticed and rarely thanked. Plan to thank one of them next Sunday. Ask God to give them strength and passion for what they do. Pray protection over them just as you would anyone else in a ministry role.

— Notes —

Just a Little Bit Crazy

*Then the Lord said to Gideon, "With the three hundred
men who lapped I will rescue you and hand over the Midianites
to you. Let everyone else go home." So the people gathered their
supplies and trumpets, and Gideon sent all the Israelites
home, but kept the three hundred.*

JUDGES 7:7-8

*T*he night wore on, but the storm showed no signs of letting up. Peter stood at the stern of the boat, tiller in hand, shouting orders at everyone. James and John were at the oars, straining to move the small craft forward against the wind and waves, and Andrew was hopping from one place to another in response to Peter's commands, trying to keep everyone and everything in the boat as it rolled from one side to the other. The others were huddled near the middle, holding on to each other and anything else they could get their hands on. Everyone was wet. Everyone was tired. It was three a.m.

Thomas glanced back toward the unseen shoreline they had left hours ago and wondered about suggesting they turn back. His thoughts froze. He screamed; his cry piercing through the din of the storm. The others' eyes followed his past the stern to the figure of a man walking over the water in their direction. Fear seized them. Peter, whose eyes were still focused ahead, swore at them, understanding the extreme peril they were in from the storm. Andrew wordlessly pointed a shaking hand aft. Peter glanced back, gasped, and dropped to his knees, unable to control his aching muscles.

A voice floated across the water. "Calm down. It's just me. Don't be afraid." Their tired eyes strained to make out who it was. It sounded like Jesus, but how could that be? Peter forced himself to his feet. "Lord, if that is you, ask me to come to you on the water." Jesus smiled, shaking his head slightly. "Come," he said.

Most of us heard this story for the first time as children. We know that Peter gets out of the boat and walks toward Jesus, but then loses heart and begins to sink. Jesus reaches out and saves him. Peter had to be a little crazy to let those words come out of his mouth, and a little crazier to act on them.

I would submit that our faith has become too sane. We have studied it, analyzed it, and figured it out. We know what we are supposed to say, and what we are supposed to do to stay in the boat. We want to look the part and act the part, but occasionally Jesus wants us to be just a little bit crazy, to get out of that boat and walk to him on the water.

The Bible is full of people doing crazy things for God. Noah built an ark where there was no water. Abraham left home to go somewhere, but

God didn't tell him where. Moses obeyed a voice from a burning bush. Gideon led 300 against 300,000. The apostles faced persecution and death with joy.

The life Jesus calls us to is a life on the water. It's a little bit crazy. It takes a belief in him without proof. It requires sacrifice without immediate reward. Our obedience could lead to ruin. It could lead to death. Who takes those kinds of risks? Who lives that kind of life? Crazy people do, that's who. People who are just crazy enough to follow Jesus.

Those who have gone before us have given us the example, beginning with Jesus, who set everything aside to obey the Father and bring us into the family. Right now, there are 35,000 or so cross-cultural, kingdom workers from the United States making sacrifices daily to continue the legacy. Is Jesus asking you to consider joining them? Are you that crazy?!

Questions for Reflection

1. What other examples of "crazy" can you think of in Scripture?

   _____

   _____

   _____

2. How easily do you do things that get you out of your comfort zone? What does it usually take to motivate you?

   _____

   _____

   _____

3. Is there a line you would not cross, or something you would not give up, if God clearly led you to?

   _____

   _____

   _____

Pray for the Kingdom

Today spend your time in prayer for the leaders of your city. Our guess is that you will need to do a little research on this one, because many of us don't know who our civic leaders are. Pray for your mayor and your city council. Ask God that he would move in and through them, that they would have his wisdom in making decisions. Ask that he would lead them to more Christlike principles of leadership.

Notes

What Will Obedience Cost Me?

Jesus answered, "Whoever loves me will keep my word. My
Father will love them, and we will come to them and make our
home with them. Whoever doesn't love me doesn't keep my words.
The word that you hear isn't mine. It is the word of the Father who sent me."

JOHN 14:23-24

W hat is it about obedience? Why is it such a big deal? I am caught up in the obedience thing because of what Jesus said to his followers during his last meal with them: "If you love me, obey me." That seems straightforward, and we want to be people who are marked by loving Jesus! That is why it is such a big deal.

Before we go on to what this obedience will cost us, what is it that Jesus asks us to do? First, "Love each other as I loved you" (see John 13:34), and second, "Go everywhere and encourage others to follow me like you do" (see Matthew 28:19).

These are two of the last things Jesus told his followers to do. He may ask other things of you, but let's just try to wrap our minds around these two. As we do you will see the cost of obedience quite clearly.

"Love each other as I have loved you."

How did Jesus love us? Paul described it this way in Romans 5:8: "God acted out his love for us by sacrificing Jesus, his only Son, on the cross to redeem us from the enemy's control" (my paraphrase). TIME-OUT! That would mean we need to be willing to give up the thing most dear to us to repair a relationship with someone who consistently spits in our face. Too hard? Most of us struggle with sacrificing something for our friends, much less our enemies! Maybe the other one is easier ...

"Go everywhere and encourage others to follow me like you do."

Going involves leaving—leaving everything—to take the grace of God to every kind of person all over the world. Some people, lots of people, have tried to do this, and many were killed by the people with whom they were trying to share that "good news." They made the ultimate sacrifice for their obedience.

Basically, what Jesus is asking us to do is lay everything on the altar for him, to demonstrate that we love him by following just these two commands. Give up everything—all that we have, and maybe even our very lives.

Who can do that?

None of us can in our own strength, to be honest. Even the best of us hold things back. God must come through for us. Thankfully, he usually doesn't ask us to give it all up at once, right now. He lays out baby steps for us, asking us to trust him in this or give up that. As we have courage to take one step, he lays out another.

Sometimes we succeed. Sometimes we fail. He is gracious.

Bottom line: obedience will cost you everything, but be encouraged ... nothing was really yours to begin with!

Questions for Reflection

1. Begin by taking some time to reflect on what Christ has done for us. What did he give up? How much did it cost him to love us?

   _____

   _____

2. Think of someone in your life who is hard to love. What would it take to show them that you truly loved them? What would need to change in your heart before you could even answer that question?

   _____

   _____

3. If you were to go to the ends of the earth to advance the kingdom, what would be the hardest thing for you to sacrifice along the way?

   _____

   _____

Spend your time in prayer today praying for your state government leaders. Pray for your governor and your state legislators. As with yesterday, it may take a little research to learn their names. Ask God to use them for his glory whether they acknowledge him or not. Pray that they may represent their people well and that your entire state would move toward kingdom principles.

— *Notes* —

When God Says No

Then he went a short distance farther and fell to the ground. He
prayed that, if possible, he might be spared the time of suffering. He said,
"Abba, Father, for you all things are possible. Take this cup of suffering
from me. However—not what I want but what you want."

MARK 14:35-36

*S*ometimes there is a temptation to think that just because we respond in obedience or get involved in doing something globally great for God, he will always open the storehouses of heaven and an abundance of "yes" answers will pour forth. As much as we might like that to be true, it normally isn't. As hard as we try to figure out the whys to God's answers to prayer, whether yes or no, the reasoning and explanations are elusive at best.

Cross-cultural workers wonder about these things too. Here are some of our head-scratchers:

1. Joe and Jane Smith are the perfect candidates. They tick every box when it comes to being fit for cross-cultural involvement. But as they pray, expect, and seek God for funding, it doesn't come.

2. Mary has been working among an unreached people group for a decade. She diligently grows relationships, and she and her ministry partners bathe them in prayer. To her knowledge, not one of them has yet taken steps toward the kingdom.

3. The team in Romania hears of a great need and opportunity for ministry in neighboring Moldova. They begin to seek God's face for the provision of people and funds to meet that critical need. No such provision of people or funds happens, and the door closes.

The truth is that God even told his own Son no at a crucial point, and we should all be extremely thankful for that answer. You know the story: Jesus is in the garden praying and agonizing to the point of sweat "like drops of blood" (Luke 22:44). He asks his Father to find another way, saying, "for you all things are possible" (Mark 14:36). Jesus then resigns himself to suffer and die according to his Father's will, and we are co-heirs with him as a result.

As difficult as it is to wrap our brains around it, here is the challenge:

"Ask whatever you will, in my name, and it will be done for you" and "Not my will but yours be done" have to fit into the same space in reality. In obedience, we continue to pray, trusting that God will follow through with the best answer, though our definition of "best" will no doubt differ from his in many cases.

Global kingdom growth is God's aim, and ultimately he is responsible for how it plays out. Our obedience allows us to be involved for his glory and pleasure—and our joy.

> Let my thoughts be thy thoughts
> Our spirits be one
> Let my will be thy will
> And thy will be done

Questions for Reflection

1. How have you experienced God in obedience and blessing?

2. Why do you think that God answers "yes" to some requests and "no" to others?

3. Are you willing to follow him in obedience even when his answers are "no" or "wait" to things we believe are important to us and our success?

Pray for the Kingdom

Today pray for the emergency response personnel in your city, the first responders who come to the aid of those who are weak and in greatest need. Ask that God would protect them and empower them to save lives. Thank God for their families who are at risk of losing a father or mother, son or daughter, each day they go on duty for our sake. Pray for their safety and welfare.

Notes

Passion Without Action Is Dead

My brothers and sisters, what good is it if people say they have faith
but do nothing to show it? Claiming to have faith can't save anyone, can
it? Imagine a brother or sister who is naked and never has enough food to eat.
What if one of you said, "Go in peace! Stay warm! Have a nice meal!"? What
good is it if you don't actually give them what their body needs? In the same
way, faith is dead when it doesn't result in faithful activity. Someone might
claim, "You have faith and have action." But how can I see your faith
apart from your actions? Instead, I'll show you my faith by
putting it into practice in faithful action.

JAMES 2:14-18

ecently I was watching New Life Worship performing "Great I Am" by Jared Anderson. This is a wonderful song, full of honor and glory and praise for the King. During the video the camera panned around the congregation, showing a very passionate group of people pouring themselves out emotionally before their God.

As my wife and I travel for work, we have been privileged to be part of such worship experiences. On one occasion, we were visiting a church in the Los Angeles area whose speaking pastor had just returned from a short-term mission experience somewhere. He was changed, no doubt, as he could neither put words to what he had experienced, nor steps to what he should do now. At the end of his message he asked the five hundred twenty-somethings gathered there how many would follow Jesus to the ends of the earth. Everyone in the place stood to their feet, raising their hands and verbally responding as one person. It was moving.

We found ourselves sitting there afterward, as everyone returned to their usual, casual selves, thinking, *What now?* Emotions had been high, and passions were being poured out like water before the King ... but what now? There were no steps to take. There was no action out of that passion. It seemed to die within the echoes inside the worship hall.

When will our passion result in action? When will it
spill out of our hallowed halls and onto the streets outside?

Passion is so much more easily expressed in community, when emotions mesh and risk is low. Boiling passion down to "doing" in the real world becomes work, the kind of work that requires the commitment of time, energy, and money. It's not a popular topic. But these are the kinds of sacrifices that are required for kingdom growth. Passion must be put into action.

Just how far will your passion take you?

What if God required of you what you promised him while within the four walls of a church building or while praying quietly and alone? What if the words you sing every Sunday were promises to God of your commitment to him? What will your answer be when he whispers, "Who can we send? Who will go for us?" My guess is that you will answer, "Here am I. Send me." When you do, get ready to put action to your words of commitment.

Obedience cannot be accomplished by passion alone.

Questions for Reflection

1. Take time to think of the lyrics of your favorite worship songs. What kinds of things have you been singing to God in worship? Are you ready to act on those promises?

   _____

   _____

   _____

2. What would it take for you to put action to your passion? What would be the first step?

   _____

   _____

   _____

3. How are you living your faith today? What "works" are results of your faith?

   _____

   _____

   _____

Pray for the Kingdom

Pray for our military today. They, like first responders, put their lives in harm's way for our safety. Pray for their families—their mothers and fathers, spouses, and children. Thank God for them. Ask God to give them wisdom about when to act and when to wait. Ask him to bring those who are away safely home.

Notes

The Chosen

"So get going. I'm sending you to Pharaoh
to bring my people, the Israelites, out of Egypt."

But Moses said to God, "Who am I to go to
Pharaoh and to bring the Israelites out of Egypt?"
EXODUS 3:10-11

*H*ave you ever been in one of those playground team-picking scenarios?

I think, in picking teams, it's best to be picked in the middle. Expectations are high for the first chosen, but no one wants to be picked last either. Middle is good enough. Just good enough.

But just good enough doesn't cut it in the kingdom, and the people who may appear the least qualified— like you may feel— may be God's best for the job!

Consider Saul of Tarsus

Saul was a Jew, but he grew up outside of Israel, so he was also a Roman citizen. He went to the best schools and had a trade. Saul was a driven person and had the mental chops to argue most people into submission, so he probably wasn't always too fun to be around. In addition, he had a fanatical devotion to God and was willing to apply that devotion to the extent of sending people to their death.

The people we are referring to here were followers of "the Way," a radical group of Jews who adhered to the teachings of a rogue rabbi named Jesus, whom they claimed was the promised Messiah. He had been killed, but they were convinced that Jesus had been raised from the dead. And people thought Saul was a fanatic!

Saul would not be on anyone's list of potential kingdom workers. He was, in fact, an enemy of the cross, a persecutor of the Way. Staying off Saul's radar was a life goal!

God saw Saul differently.

God knew that Saul was just who he needed to take the kingdom to the next level. Here is what God says about Saul to Ananias, when asking him to restore Saul's sight:

> The Lord replied, "Go! This man is the agent I have chosen to
> carry my name before Gentiles, kings, and Israelites. I will show
> him how much he must suffer for the sake of my name."

ACTS 9:15-16

Saul was chosen by God to introduce the gospel to the world at that time. What about us? What about you? Do you feel unqualified? Are we telling God, "Please don't send me," or are we willing to be God's chosen ones to proclaim his name to our friends, our acquaintances, our enemies, and the rest of the people in the world?

We each say, "I am not ..."
God says, "I AM."

Questions for Reflection

1. Do you see yourself in Moses? Have there been times when you felt totally incapable of what God was asking?

_____

_____

2. How did you handle those times? What was your response to God?

_____

_____

3. If you have said no to God, what were the results? What happens when we say yes to God?

_____

_____

Pray for the Kingdom

Pray for our president today, whether you agree with their politics or not. Pray that God will use them for good and not evil. Pray that God will protect them and reveal himself to them in a new way today. Also pray that they will respond to God's leading, whether they recognize it as him or not, and lead our country in a way that is pleasing and glorifying to God.

— *Notes* —

When It's Okay to Be God

*Adopt the attitude that was in Christ Jesus: Though he was in the form
of God, he did not consider being equal with God something to exploit. But
he emptied himself by taking the form of a slave and by becoming like human
beings. When he found himself in the form of a human, he humbled himself
by becoming obedient to the point of death, even death on a cross.*

PHILIPPIANS 2:5-8

*O*ne of the great criticisms of our current generation, especially in the U.S., is that we have an ingrained desire to be God to ourselves. Most believers would consider this a condition handed down to us from the very beginning, as part of the original "fall." The serpent offered the first family the chance to "be like God, knowing good and evil" (Genesis 3:5). They accepted the offer, and we have been chasing after that chance ever since.

Being God to ourselves is something to avoid but being *Jesus* to *someone else* is something we should be all about. We should always have an answer for the "Where is God when ...?" question, because God indwells us. God is there in every situation, good or horrible, for each of us. No one should ever have to wonder about the presence of God when they are with us. If God's presence within us isn't obvious, then maybe we are not being clear in our representation of him.

Asking "What would Jesus do?" is so yesterday, or maybe even so last millennium, but it remains a good question to ask ourselves as people around us face crisis. Maybe we should restate that question as, "How can I be Jesus in someone's life today?" or "What does love require of me today?"

Living the answer to those questions is the essence of being on mission, being missional, or being a missionary in all contexts. Living the answer to those questions draws us away from *spiritual platitudes*, well-meaning but empty phrases about God's goodness or presence or control or ultimate victory, which come quickly to mind and are easily said. Words are easy to use because they don't require action on our part. We can skate by, saying, "Be warm and be filled," as the writer of James (see James 2:16) reflects, so we know it isn't a new challenge.

> Don't do anything for selfish purposes, but with humility think
> of others as better than yourselves. Instead of each person watching
> out for their own good, watch out for what is better for others.
>
> PHILIPPIANS 2:3-4

Asking what Jesus would do leads us into action. When someone is hurting, they need to be given love, not just words about a loving God.

Is living this way easy? Not at all. Not even a little bit. Some of us are better at it than others. Being the hands and feet of Jesus to someone requires that we sacrifice being what we want to be in those situations. We must sacrifice ourselves to meet the needs of others. Expend ourselves to feed them when they are hungry. Pour ourselves out to give them drink when they are thirsty.

Love, in its truest form, always requires sacrifice.

Being God to ourselves and being God to someone else are exact opposites. The former is our natural bent. The latter is our supernatural commission. Jesus said it this way: "This is my commandment: love each other just as I have loved you" (John 15:12).

And how did Jesus love us? He loved us to death, literally.

Questions for Reflection

1. How do you feel after reading this? Overwhelmed? Incapable?

   _____

   _____

2. How can you learn to love like Christ? What resources do you have?

   _____

   _____

3. How would you like to be loved by someone else, if they were to love you like Christ?

   _____

   _____

   _____

Pray for the members of Congress today on both sides of the aisle. Ask that God would give them his wisdom to govern well. Ask that they might put aside differences and make the good of the people their first priority. Thank God for them and ask him to bless them. Pray especially for the congressmen and women from your state. Ask that God would empower them to do good for the people around you.

— Notes —

Are You Enough?

You are the one who created my innermost parts;
you knit me together while I was still in my mother's womb.
I give thanks to you that I was marvelously set apart.
Your works are wonderful—I know that very well.
My bones weren't hidden from you
when I was being put together in a secret place,
when I was being woven together in the deep parts of the earth.
Your eyes saw my embryo,
and on your scroll every day was written that was being formed for me,
before any one of them had yet happened.
God, your plans are incomprehensible to me!
Their total number is countless!
If I tried to count them—they outnumber grains of sand!
If I came to the very end—I'd still be with you.

PSALM 139:13-18

*M*any of these reflections focus on calls to action in obedience to the Jesus' Great Commission. In all of that it would be possible to feel overwhelmed, first by the need—but also by how small we are—how inadequate we are—in the face of that need. We are tempted to cry out, "Lord, what I have to offer isn't enough, not even a drop of water in the bottomless, thirsty cup of the world."

To be blunt, this is a lie of the enemy. His tactic from the beginning has been to make us feel as if we need something more than God. We believed him then, and we believe him now.

YOU ARE ENOUGH. God made you enough for what he is leading you to do. All God needs is you, just as you are, with just what you have to offer. God has told us this over and over in Scripture, but we doubt him just as often as we believe the enemy.

YOU ARE ENOUGH. For some reason our all-powerful God has chosen, and apparently loves, to use us in our weakness. He told the apostle Paul, "My grace is enough for you, for it is in your imperfect weakness that I am perfectly strong" (2 Corinthians 12:9, my paraphrase). Paul was asking that God take away the weakness, the "thorn in his flesh," that was limiting him in the work he was so passionately pursuing. In effect God said, "No, Paul. That is actually when I do my best work—when you can't rely on yourself and are forced to depend on me."

YOU ARE ENOUGH. Your two fish and five pieces of bread can feed thousands in the hands of Jesus. All that is necessary is to offer them to be used by him. The impossible not only becomes *possible*, but becomes *reality* in Jesus.

YOU ARE ENOUGH. Your doubting, denying, and failure are not new to God. He remembers that we are only dirt— but dirt shaped by him and gifted by him with the breath of life.

YOU ARE ENOUGH. Just you ... just who you are ... just the way you are ... with just what you possess to give. Lose your weakness in his strength.

Lose your doubt in his assurance. Lose your inadequacy in his sufficiency. Lose your despair in his hope. Lose your hate in his love.

May I get lost in your living
Lost in the smile on your face
When I get lost in the depths of you
I'm found within your grace

You are enough.

Questions for Reflection

1. When do you feel most inadequate? What leads you to those places?

   _____

   _____

   _____

2. How do you truly feel God thinks about you? Do you really believe he loves you?

   _____

   _____

   _____

3. What is one thing about yourself that you can thank God for right now?

   _____

   _____

   _____

Pray for the Kingdom

Pray for the Supreme Court today. Go online and find a list of the justices and pray for them by name. Ask God to give them his wisdom as they consider some of the most important legal cases in the country. Ask God to allow them to put personal preferences aside and seek the best for the people of this country. Thank God for each of them and ask him to bless them.

Notes

Intersections and Kingdom Growth

An angel from the Lord spoke to Philip, "At noon, take the road
that leads from Jerusalem to Gaza." (This is a desert road.) So he did.
Meanwhile, an Ethiopian man was on his way home from
Jerusalem, where he had come to worship.

ACTS 8:26-27A

*M*aybe you have watched the movie *The Martian*, which stars Matt Damon as an astronaut who gets stranded on Mars. His rescue hangs on a thin thread—the nearly impossible intersection of his spacecraft with his teammates' ship orbiting the red planet. The tension makes for a great story.

All our lives are a series of similar hit-or-miss intersections,
but most of them occur without our understanding
or awareness of them.

God, though, is not unaware. He is the master of "circumstantial" meetings, and Scripture is full of such stories. One of my favorites is the account of Joseph who is in prison and meets up with none other than the cupbearer to Pharaoh.

Joseph had been in the prison for some time, and because of his faithfulness and God's favor, had grown into a kind of leadership in that dark and hopeless place. Pharaoh must have been in a difficult mood one day, because he sent both his butler (cupbearer) and his baker to the same prison. No doubt, Joseph became known to them. Not long after they had arrived, they each had dreams, and Joseph was able to interpret the dreams. The butler would be reinstated, the baker would be killed. The butler promises to tell Pharaoh about Joseph but forgets until Pharaoh himself has a dream. Joseph is "redeemed" from prison and placed in a position of authority from which he eventually saves the lives of his entire clan.

What intersections is God leading you to today? Will you have your eyes open to see them?

We seem to live our lives as if such meetings are random.
What if they aren't?

What if God intended for you to meet the people you do because you are at a specific step along their path and he wants you to connect with them?

Would you act differently knowing that?

Maybe we should assume that each intersection with someone has a God component—one of *sowing, watering, weeding,* or *reaping*—instead of assuming it is just a chance meeting.

A commitment to be like Jesus in every interaction is probably too much to jump into headfirst, so work your way into it. Today, try to change the way you see the intersections of your life with others. Awareness is the best, first step.

As a second step, try to be sensitive to the leading of the Holy Spirit and his intentions for those people. Ask deeper questions. Listen intently to their answers; what are they truly saying and what are they purposely not saying?

Dare to go deeper with the people around you. Let them into who you authentically are. The more real you are with others the more willingly they will be real with you, and you will see doors open to be impacted and to have impact.

Your next intersection could change the course of your life, the life of the person you meet, and the growth of the kingdom.

Questions for Reflection

1. How aware have you been that each "intersection" during your day may be a kingdom one?

   _____

   _____

2. How have you used those encounters before?

   _____

   _____

3. What might you do to be more sensitive to God's intentions for those "random" meetings?

   _____

   _____

Pray for the health, growth, and multiplication of the kingdom of God in the United States today. Ask that God will move through his Spirit and through his people to bring about change in our country through love, a love that reflects Jesus and his love for us. Pray that we all, as his people and ambassadors, will commit ourselves to loving each other, because that will identify us as his people and bring glory to him!

Notes

I See You

*A man with a skin disease approached Jesus, fell to his knees,
and begged, "If you want, you can make me clean."*

*[Filled with compassion], Jesus reached out his hand,
touched him, and said, "I do want to. Be clean." Instantly,
the skin disease left him, and he was clean.*

MARK 1:40-42

*S*o often we get to the end of a day and realize that we have not truly engaged with anyone on a level deeper than a nod. How often have you been asked, "How are you?" and your response was, "Fine"? Maybe you added, "How are you?" and you got the response, "Doing well." Neither you nor the other person expected anything different. In most cases, we don't have the desire to really learn how someone is doing. One of the criticisms of the technology generation is that our virtual connections are shallow. One might question if this type of face-to-face communication we participate in every day is any better.

In many cultures, greetings and leave-takings are of much greater importance. For instance, if we were in a Zulu-speaking area of southern Africa we would be greeted with the word *sawubona. Sawubona,* which literally means "We see you," carries with it a deeper understanding: *we know you ... we understand and respect you ... you have meaning for us.*

What if we were to commit to live *sawubona* lives each day?

What if we were to greet and treat each person we met with a deeper commitment to know and understand them, relate to them, and engage them where they are? How would that change their day? How would that change our day?

An interesting fact about Jesus is that though he was God in human form, people did not feel judged by him. They flocked to him. Mobbed him. He was considered "a friend of sinners." In fact, the only people who felt uneasy around Jesus were the religious people, because he didn't fit into the religious patterns they had set up— the patterns they thought defined being godlike. If Jesus were truly a prophet, or the Messiah, as he claimed, wouldn't he be more holy, set apart, and perfect? How could he allow himself to be soiled by hanging around with known sinners and traitors?

What made the difference? Could it have been that Jesus took the time to live out *sawubona* in his relationships? Though that word didn't exist at the time, a similar Hebrew word did: שָׁלוֹם or *shalom. Shalom* carries with it a wish for peace, harmony, wholeness, completeness, prosperity, welfare, and tranquility for the person greeted. It is a word of shared community and blessing. Everyone should live in the shalom of God.

Our passion at One Challenge is to see entire nations transformed. Nations are transformed as their cities are changed. Cities are changed because of transformed communities, and communities move forward because the people in them are transformed by the gospel. People can transform into the likeness of Jesus as they are shown the likeness of Jesus by others. Living lives of *sawubona* and *shalom* can be the first step toward seeing that transformation become a reality.

In the words of Mahatma Gandhi,
"Be the change you wish to see in the world."

Questions for Reflection

1. How would your greetings change if you lived out sawubona in them?

2. How would your life change if others greeted you the same way?

3. In what ways would your relationships change if you made choices based on wanting shalom for the other person?

Pray for the rest of North America today: Canada and Mexico. Both countries are vast, and though the light of the gospel is present, there are still unreached people resident there. Pray for revival in the church that exists and a willingness to work together to see every person have a witness to the love of Jesus. Pray for the missionaries in those countries, that God would use them in significant ways to advance the kingdom.

Notes

To the Death

[Jesus] *asked a third time, "Simon son of John, do you love me?"*

Peter was sad that Jesus asked him a third time, "Do you love me?"
He replied, "Lord, you know everything; you know I love you."

Jesus said to him, "Feed my sheep. I assure you that when you
were younger you tied your own belt and walked around wherever you
wanted to. When you grow old, you will stretch out your hands and another
will tie your belt and lead you where you don't want to go." He said this
to show the kind of death by which Peter would glorify God.
After saying this, Jesus said to Peter, "Follow me."
JOHN 21:17-19

ne of the most impacting images from the Disney version of the Chronicles of Narnia series comes near the end of *The Lion, the Witch and the Wardrobe.* Peter, the soon-to-be High King of Narnia, and his followers are facing the much larger forces of the White Witch in a battle for Narnia and its future. As they watch the advancing forces and prepare to charge, Peter asks the centaur next to him, "Are you with me?" The centaur answers without hesitation or reservation, "To the death." The centaur does "die" in the battle protecting Peter but is restored to life by Aslan after the victory.

"Are you with me?"

"To the death!"

Is our commitment to Jesus so deep that we will follow him without question? Wherever he may lead? However dark the way? No matter what the personal cost?

Pledging allegiance to a king is foreign to us in the United States. We often see ourselves as the masters of our own fate. We have rights. We highly value individualism and equality.

But the kingdom of God is not a democracy. It is a monarchy, and we, as subjects of that kingdom, own nothing. Everything we have is a gift from the King who owns all things, even our very lives. We serve at the whim of our Lord and Master, for his honor and glory. Even Jesus, God in the flesh, made himself subject to his Father's will, for his glory and for our sakes. Should we be willing to offer any less?

In the sacrifice of Jesus, we have become heirs, along with him, of the kingdom of God. But heirs, though beloved, are not exempt from sacrifice for the king or their kingdom. We can visualize this from another movie, *The Fellowship of the Ring,* from the *Lord of the Rings* series. At the counsel of Elrond where the fellowship of the ring is formed, Frodo has just offered to be the ring bearer and Aragorn, the rightful king and heir of Gondor, responds by pledging himself to Frodo. He says, "If by my life or my death I can protect you, I will." Some things are more important than life itself.

Most of us will never face the opportunity to lay down our lives for the kingdom, but we should day by day grow in our willingness to lay down those things we hold onto upon the altar as living sacrifices to our King. It was he who laid himself down on the altar for us.

This is not easy, and it will take a lifetime of effort, but it is a worthy quest, and one that will make us more like our King each day.

**Make a commitment to listen for what the Spirit
living in you would prompt you to do each day and,
to the best of who you are, respond in obedience.**

"After all, he's not a tame lion."
"No, but he is good."

Questions for Reflection

1. What things are you holding onto that would keep you from responding "To the death" if Jesus should ask if you are with him?

2. Who in your life are you willing to die for?

3. Who are you not willing to die for? Do you realize that Jesus died for that person?

Pray for the Kingdom

Pray for Central America today. The countries in Central America are Guatemala, Belize, El Salvador, Honduras, Nicaragua, Costa Rica, and Panama. These countries are small, and missionaries have been working there for over a hundred years. As a result, the church is growing and is sending missionaries to other parts of Latin America and all over the world. Praise God for that maturity and ask for continued growth and commitment for the believers there. Pray for the pastors of churches, that they would continue to openly share the gospel and that those who need more training and education would be able to receive it. Pray also for the missionary movement from Central America to other parts of the world.

Notes

Life Is Good

*I was very glad in the Lord because now at last you have shown
concern for me again. (Of course you were always concerned but had
no way to show it.) I'm not saying this because I need anything, for I have
learned how to be content in any circumstance. I know the experience of being
in need and of having more than enough; I have learned the secret to being
content in any and every circumstance, whether full or hungry or
whether having plenty or being poor. I can endure all these things
through the power of the one who gives me strength.*

PHILIPPIANS 4:10-13

Life is good … until it's bad.

Life is easy … until it's hard.

All of us realize at some point or another that things don't always turn out the way we would hope. In fact, sometimes they turn out horribly. There is no need to get specific or give examples. Everyone reading this could share at least one experience. If you're having trouble agreeing with this, just watch the news tonight. Horrible things are happening all around us.

How confusing it can be when things that seem so right to us turn out so wrong. We are reminded that we cannot see the road ahead. We cannot know the mind of God. His ways are higher than our ways, and his thoughts are beyond our wildest imagination. We trust his Word when it says that he is good and that he is able to bring "all things together for good for the ones who love God, for those who are called according to his purpose" (Romans 8:28). Jesus told us we would suffer in this world. He also told us to be encouraged because he has overcome the world (see John 16:33).

We can determine, to the best of our ability and strength, how we respond to the life path God has laid out for us. A seasoned mission worker once said, "You can't control what happens to you, but you can always control what happens *through* you." Our attitudes are a choice. We choose whether to be thankful or complain.

So how should we react when facing what is before us—today, next week, or twenty years from now?

We should receive every circumstance as an opportunity:

… to praise God.

… to glorify God.

… to trust God.

… to see God.

… to become more like God.

This does not mean that we don't struggle or question.

Job did. David did. Paul did. Even Jesus did, in the garden before his crucifixion. What this does mean is that we can come out on the other side closer to God, with a better understanding of who he is and who we are in him. Whether we like it or not, we grow when we go through hard times.

Life on mission, whether in your own culture or while living and working in a different culture, is a life lived reflecting Christ in and through every circumstance. Will we do that perfectly? Of course not. Can we do better than we are doing now? Undoubtedly.

Questions for Reflection

1. When you have faced disappointment with God in the past, how have you dealt with it?

   _____

   _____

   _____

2. Who do you turn to when what is happening around you makes no spiritual sense?

   _____

   _____

   _____

3. Do you feel you can be honest with God about your doubts?

   _____

   _____

   _____

Pray for the Kingdom

Pray for South America today. The countries of South America are Argentina, Bolivia, Brazil, Chile, Colombia, Ecuador, French Guiana, Guyana, Paraguay, Peru, Suriname, Uruguay, and Venezuela. Though most of these countries would be considered "reached" by researchers, there are certainly still unreached people groups in the Amazon. Many of these countries are sending missionaries to other parts of the world, with Brazil having the third-most missionaries of all countries (behind the U.S. and South Korea). Pray for continued support of the missionary effort and for revival in the church that exists.

Notes

What I Do Today Matters

You are the salt of the earth. But if salt loses its saltiness, how will it
become salty again? It's good for nothing except to be thrown away and
trampled under people's feet. You are the light of the world. A city on top of a
hill can't be hidden. Neither do people light a lamp and put it under a basket.
Instead, they put it on top of a lampstand, and it shines on all who are in the
house. In the same way, let your light shine before people, so they can see
the good things you do and praise your Father who is in heaven.

MATTHEW 5:13-16

*O*ur One Challenge Prepare for Impact team loves Donald Miller's *Building a StoryBrand* podcast. On one episode Miller interviewed golfer Ben Crane, who made a statement that stood out to us:

"What I do today matters."

If you stopped reading right now but remembered that one thing—that what you do today matters—you will have taken a huge step toward making an impact in your world.

It reminds me of the final scene of *Mr. Holland's Opus,* in which Mr. Holland feels he has wasted his life on teaching instead of becoming a successful composer. In the midst of that disappointment, he learns that he has indeed become a successful composer, and the symphony he has composed was written into the lives of the people he impacted—his students.

What you do today matters. Ben Crane's statement applies to all areas of life. Decisions we make today bring about the circumstances we face tomorrow. Said another way, your desires for the future should dictate the choices you make today. Many of us enjoy watching the Olympics. The success those athletes achieve relates directly to the choices and sacrifices they have made over the last four or more years. What if we had the same commitment for the growth of the kingdom? What if we decided today to bypass a five-dollar latte to give five dollars to some kingdom cause?

What you do today matters. It is possible that you are thinking, "What good would five dollars do?" You're right, five dollars won't do much, but what if half of the Christ-followers in the United States decided to give five dollars toward the kingdom? According to Pew Research Center, there are just over 76 million evangelicals in the U.S. If 38 million of them each gave a one-time, five-dollar gift it would result in $190 million for the kingdom. Our agency is a mid-sized mission agency with a yearly budget of around $14 million. That one-time gift of five dollars given by that many people could fund thirteen agencies our size for an entire year without our missionaries having to raise another dime!

What you do today matters. As in *Mr. Holland's Opus*, your choices today impact the lives of those around you, both those with whom you have intentional contact and those with whom you have incidental contact. Everyone you interact with today will be influenced by what you say or don't say, and by what you do or don't do. Your impact is written on people's lives, whether you realize it or not.

Be intentional today. Impact your world.
Make it better because you are in it.

Put your light on a stand so that it provides
light for everyone in the entire house.

Questions for Reflection

1. What differences would you make in your daily routine if you lived life believing that it mattered, to God and to those around you?

   _____

   _____

   _____

2. Have you given much thought to the legacy you are leaving? What would you want it to be if you could make the choice now?

   _____

   _____

   _____

3. What things are keeping you from leaving that kind of legacy?

   _____

   _____

   _____

— Pray for the Kingdom —

Pray for western Europe today, which includes these countries: Andorra, Austria, Belgium, Czech Republic, France, Germany, Ireland, Italy, Liechtenstein, Monaco, the Netherlands, Portugal, Spain, Switzerland, and the United Kingdom. As most of you remember from your world history, at one point, Portugal and Spain controlled most of the world, and then England took over and created the largest empire in the world. Much of that expansion also spread the religion of those countries, which was predominately Christian (Catholic and Anglican). Today,y the landscape in most of these countries is dotted with Catholic, Orthodox, and Lutheran churches. The "free" churches, which are not government-sponsored, are where you find most of the spiritual light. Pray for revival in the mainline churches. Pray for encouragement and opportunity for the free churches and their pastors. Pray for a rebirth of the missions movement from churches in these countries to their neighbors and the rest of the world.

— Notes —

What It's All About

Shout triumphantly to the Lord, all the earth!
Serve the Lord with celebration!
Come before him with shouts of joy!
Know that the Lord is God—
he made us; we belong to him.
We are his people,
the sheep of his own pasture.
Enter his gates with thanks;
enter his courtyards with praise!
Thank him! Bless his name!
Because the Lord is good,
his loyal love lasts forever;
his faithfulness lasts generation after generation.

PSALM 100

*I*t might seem ambitious of me to think I might know what it's all about, but I have a take on it:

It's all about worship!

Where everything is going and where it all ends up is **worship**. Don't believe me? Read Revelation 5:11-14:

Then I looked, and I heard the sound of many angels surrounding
the throne, the living creatures, and the elders. They numbered in the millions—
thousands upon thousands. They said in a loud voice,

"Worthy is the slaughtered Lamb to receive power, wealth,
wisdom, and might, and honor, glory, and blessing."

And I heard every creature in heaven and on earth and under
the earth and in the sea—I heard everything everywhere say,

"Blessing, honor, glory, and power belong to the one seated
on the throne and to the Lamb forever and always."

Then the four living creatures said, "Amen,"
and the elders fell down and worshipped.

John Piper once said, "Missions is not the ultimate goal of the church. Worship is. Missions exists because worship doesn't."

Want to live for the kingdom? Live a life of worship.

Often, we live like worship relates only to part of a "worship service" or the music that happens at the church we attend. That is part of it, but far from the complete story. Living worship is focusing every thought, every word, and every act on bringing glory to God. The apostle Paul put it this way in his letter to the Christ-followers in Rome:

So, brothers and sisters, because of God's mercies, I encourage you
to present your bodies as a living sacrifice that is holy and pleasing to God.
This is your appropriate priestly service. Don't be conformed to the patterns of
this world, but be transformed by the renewing of your minds so that you can
figure out what God's will is—what is good and pleasing and mature.

ROMANS 12:1-2

A sacrifice has one purpose. Worship. Worship should be the end result of everything we do.

Worship in everything. Everything in worship.

Questions for Reflection

1. What do you think a life lived in worship would look like for you?

2. Most of us think of worship as music. What other forms of worship can you list?

3. How would your life change if you committed more of it to worshipping God?

Pray for the Kingdom

Pray for Eastern Europe today, including a Albania, Belarus, Bosnia and Herzegovina, Bulgaria, Croatia, Estonia, Greece, Hungary, Latvia, Lithuania, Moldova, Montenegro, North Macedonia, Poland, Romania, Serbia, Slovakia, Slovenia, Ukraine, western Russia, and western Turkey. Many of these countries were part of the former Soviet Union. During that time atheism was taught in schools, and the Orthodox Church was tolerated at best, but mostly persecuted. As a result, most people in midlife have very little understanding of religion beyond seeing Orthodox churches in their towns. The Holy Spirit has been at work in a mighty way in recent years, and the church is growing. Pray for continued growth and outreach within these countries. Pray also for the missions movement of these small and growing churches. Romania seems to be leading this group of countries in sending missionaries, but the church in other places is also catching a passion for the Great Commission.

Notes

Dependency

He said to me, "My grace is enough for you, because power is
made perfect in weakness." So I'll gladly spend my time bragging
about my weaknesses so that Christ's power can rest on me. Therefore,
I'm all right with weaknesses, insults, disasters, harassments, and stressful
situations for the sake of Christ, because when I'm weak, then I'm strong.

2 CORINTHIANS 12:9-10

*D*ependency seems like an un-American word. We are proud of our independence. We hear statements like "God helps those who help themselves" and "Pull yourself up by your own bootstraps" and think they are in the Bible (but they aren't!).

It should be no surprise, then, that we are not very good at being dependent. Being dependent feels weak, and being weak is not valued in our society.

If you feel God is leading you toward cross-cultural work of some kind, you will learn about being dependent in ways you have not yet imagined—and they are rarely fun!

Dependency: If you are a financially supported missionary, you will quickly understand that you are completely dependent on the people who send money to your agency each month so that you can survive and do ministry.

Dependency: In your early days in a non-English-speaking country you may find yourself lost and realize that, unless someone who speaks English happens by, you may not make it back home. Five-year-old locals will have a better grasp of language than you.

Dependency: Your relationship with God may be the only one that is going anywhere, because he is the only one who understands you or has time for you.

Dependency: In a new place, in a culture you don't understand, you will find yourself fully dependent on those foreigners who have been there longer than you to do something as simple as catching a cab to the airport.

Let's step back for a moment and think about what it is to be a Christ-follower:
A follower depends on the leadership of the leader.
Our position with God is dependent upon God's grace for us.
The only way to produce fruit is to abide in and depend on the vine.

"Apart from me, you can do nothing."

JOHN 15:5 (NLT)

Don't wait to be forced into dependency by living and working in another country. Embrace your dependency right here, right now. Learn to be weak and dependent on God's all-sufficient power. Let him speak. You listen. Let him lead. You follow. Let him call. You answer.

Questions for Reflection

1. What are areas of your life do you feel fully competent in?

   _____

   _____

2. What are some areas of life where you feel weak?

   _____

   _____

   _____

3. What would need to happen to in order for you to take a dependent posture in every situation?

   _____

   _____

   _____

Pray for the Kingdom

Pray for the countries of northern Europe today. Those countries are Denmark, Finland, Greenland, Iceland, Norway, and Sweden. The Lutheran church is the state church in these countries, so they would be considered "reached" countries. Please pray for new life in these churches. The highest percentage of active Christ-followers is in Norway. That country along with Finland and Sweden have been instrumental in the missionary sending movement of the last century, but those numbers are shrinking and their influence waning. Pray for encouragement for local pastors and other church leaders.

Notes

Every Day Is a Gift

In the beginning was the Word and the Word
was with God and the Word was God.
The Word was with God in the beginning.
Everything came into being through the Word,
and without the Word nothing came into being.
What came into being through the Word was life,
and the life was the light for all people.
The light shines in the darkness, and the darkness doesn't extinguish the light.

JOHN 1:1-5

Every day since then has been a gift from God!"

We often hear a statement like this after a life-threatening experience. But if we clear away the clutter that fills our lives, there is no truer statement all the time.

Every day is a gift from God!

If we lived each day as if it were a fresh gift from God, would we live it differently? How would our choices change? How would we spend the time we have? Would we enjoy each experience at a deeper level? Would we show our love to our family and friends more lavishly? Would we focus more of our time and energy on things of eternal significance?

God does not owe us anything, but he has blessed us graciously with everything we have— even down to each breath that we breathe. As the apostle Paul put it when he presented the gospel in Athens, "In him we live and move and have our being" (Acts 17:28 ESV).

Jesus told the story of three servants whose master gave them money to be used while he was away on a trip. Two of them did exactly that, and when their master returned, they were rewarded. The third just buried the money. The master threw him out.

When we give a gift to someone, aren't we most happy when we see them enjoy it by using it? How do you think God feels about the way you are using the gift he has given you? As you think about this, remember that your use of this gift of each day does not change his love for you. When we as parents give gifts to our children we don't love them any less if they don't use it or enjoy it. God is the perfect example of a loving parent, and though we may not understand him fully, we can be certain of his love for us. It was demonstrated at the cross.

Will you make today a different day? Enjoy today as a gift. Use today as a gift meant to be significant for you, for others, and for the kingdom. We don't have to wait until we have a life-threatening experience to live this way.

Yesterday cannot be changed

Tomorrow can't be written

All we have is now, today
To use, to do, to live in

If this be true should we not give
More care to how we live it?
For time once spent is time now gone
We cannot apprehend it.

Every day is a gift from God. Go live the life out of today!

— Questions for Reflection —

1. How often do you get to the end of the day and feel you haven't lived it well?

   _____

   _____

   _____

2. What kinds of things would help you feel like you have lived each day to the fullest?

   _____

   _____

   _____

3. What reminders could you put in place to help you remember to live each day as a gift?

   _____

   _____

   _____

Pray for the Kingdom

Pray for the countries of the Middle East today. Tthis region includes Bahrain, Iran, Iraq, Israel, Jordan, Kuwait, Lebanon, Oman, Palestine, Qatar, Saudi Arabia, Syria, eastern Turkey, United Arab Emirates, and Yemen. All except Israel are dominated by Islam. Some of them are very wealthy because of their oil deposits, but others are very poor. There is a measure of religious freedom in Jordan and Lebanon, but in the other Islamic countries the church is persecuted. Internal conflict between Islamic sects also fills the news. Refugees from Syria and other countries have created a humanitarian crisis in Europe. Missionaries have responded, and many Muslims are coming to faith in refugee camps as a result. Pray for Israel, that its people would turn to their Messiah and seek redemption and restoration in the new kingdom of God, the kingdom ushered in by Jesus. Pray for peace and the opportunity for the gospel to have greater effect.

Notes

Who Are You Leading?

So now, revere the Lord. Serve him honestly and faithfully.
Put aside the gods that your ancestors served beyond the Euphrates
and in Egypt and serve the Lord. But if it seems wrong in your opinion to
serve the Lord, then choose today whom you will serve. Choose the gods whom
your ancestors served beyond the Euphrates or the gods of the Amorites in
whose land you live. But my family and I will serve the Lord.
JOSHUA 24:14-15

*W*hether we realize it or not, we are leaders. Someone is listening to our comments (personally or virtually), following our advice, or watching and being influenced by our example. Leadership is not something that can be avoided. Leadership is a reality.

Who are you leading and how are you doing at it?

Some roles of leader and follower are clearly defined, so evaluating our performance is clear and obvious. Mentoring, coaching, teaching, and parenting are examples of obvious roles of influence. Some roles, however, are less evident. Social media may be the most influential leadership medium of the current generation, but most of us don't think about how the comments we make on social media are influencing others. Maybe we should, though, because we even refer to our contacts on social media as "followers"!

I am sure that most of us recall news stories about bullying in educational settings. Bullying is not new, but its effect on lives today, through the instant and widespread influence of social media, has brought about devastating results. The number of children and young adults who have considered suicide, some of them following through with it, is just not acceptable. Bullying is a form of the dark side of leadership, and its power to control and motivate is clear. Don't think that the church is free from this evil. We carry out a form of bullying in judging others, whether inside the church or outside of it. Jesus commanded us to love each other, love our neighbors, and even love our enemies. There is no place for judgment or bullying in God's kingdom, which is defined by love.

Live your life with care because others, seen and unseen, are being influenced by watching you.

When you take the leap to cross-cultural work and ministry, you increase the visibility of your leadership and influence, especially in places where you are clearly an outsider. People will relate to you based on your cultural background, and you will impact their opinion about your home culture by the way you live. When unfounded stories about adoptions of Guatemalan children leading to the harvesting of baby parts for transplants circulated in that country, missionaries from North America were immediately suspect. On the opposite side, disrespecting your host culture by openly talking down its ways of living will have an impact on the people in your sphere, and they will project that onto all visitors from your culture. If you have children and disrespect people in their presence, how do you think they will feel about those people?

Take your leadership seriously in your home culture or in a host culture, whether in obvious leadership roles or those less evident. Live your life on purpose, with intentionality, realizing the impact of your thoughts, words, and actions on those around you. Whether you acknowledge it or not, you are an ambassador for the kingdom of God.

Lead well!

Questions for Reflection

1. Who are you following in life? What people have had an influence on you?

2. Has that influence been positive or negative?

3. Who is following you? How have you been leading them? What changes should you make to lead others in a way that brings them to a greater understanding of God's love for them?

Pray for the Kingdom

Pray for the countries of Central Asia today. These countries are Afghanistan, Kazakhstan, Kyrgyzstan, Tajikistan, Turkmenistan, and Uzbekistan. Thlis region is over 90 percent Muslim. As with other areas with a vast majority of Islamic followers, missionaries are at risk. Many have been evacuated at various times, and some have been martyred for the gospel. Pray for the small but growing number of believers in these countries, that God would give them peace and courage. Pray for the workers from other countries who are trying to help the kingdom grow there. The people in this region are generally very poor and depend a lot on agriculture to survive. Pray that God will reveal himself through meeting their physical and spiritual needs.

Notes

Leadership Involves Sacrifice

I am the good shepherd. The good shepherd lays down
his life for the sheep. When the hired hand sees the wolf coming,
he leaves the sheep and runs away. That's because he isn't the shepherd;
the sheep aren't really his. So the wolf attacks the sheep and scatters
them. He's only a hired hand and the sheep don't matter to him.

I am the good shepherd. I know my own sheep and they know me, just as the
Father knows me and I know the Father. I give up my life for the sheep.

JOHN 10:11-15

As we considered in the previous reflection, we are all leaders in some way. Someone is following you, directly or indirectly, and in light of that, you should be intentional about what you do and say. One of the realities of being a leader is sacrifice. As a leader, the welfare of your followers is your concern. The Bible gives us a great example of this in Psalm 23. Shepherds need to be great leaders because sheep are not the best followers.

> **The Lord is my shepherd; I shall not want. He makes me lie down in green pastures. He leads me beside still waters.** *(verses 1-2 ESV)*

A leader provides for the needs of the follower as a primary concern. Finding "green pastures" and "still waters" often takes time and effort, and I think we are all surprised when our "sheep" need convincing to make use of the resources we have created or found for them. But whether they appreciate our effort or not, it is still our responsibility.

> **He restores my soul. He leads me in paths of righteousness for his name's sake.** *(verse 3 ESV)*

Not only is a leader concerned about the physical welfare of the follower but also their emotional and spiritual health. Providing an environment of wholeness and peace allows followers to grow and thrive. In today's chaotic world, it takes thought and creativity to find that place.

> **Even though I walk through the valley of the shadow of death, I will fear no evil; for you are with me; your rod and your staff, they comfort me.** *(verse 4 ESV)*

Along with wholeness and peace in the emotional realm, the leader provides physical safety for the follower. Many times, this means that the leader is putting his or her own safety at risk to protect the follower. King David, a shepherd as a youth, killed a lion and a bear and no doubt routed a pack of wolves while protecting his father's sheep. Once again, our "sheep" may not appreciate the sacrifice we make, but we must make the sacrifice just the same. They are our responsibility.

You prepare a table before me in the presence of my enemies; you anoint my head with oil; my cup overflows. *(verse 5 ESV)*

At times, the leader goes overboard and provides special things for the follower. In providing a feast in rough times, honoring them, and giving extravagant gifts, leaders show followers that they have special worth and are highly valued. Everyone lives life better when they know that someone cares for and about them.

Surely goodness and mercy shall follow me all the days of my life, and I shall dwell in the house of the Lord forever. *(verse 6 ESV)*

The leader not only provides for the present needs of the follower, but also plans for their future welfare. Planning for someone's future involves sacrifice both now and later, and often that sacrifice falls to the leader.

This kind of shepherd leadership is a lifestyle—one of sacrifice for the welfare of those around us. Let's be honest, most of us are not naturally good at this. Pray that God would help you grow into the leader he wants you to be. What seems impossible to man is possible in God!

Questions for Reflection

1. How are you leading others to places of rest and refreshment—places where their daily needs are met?

   _____

   _____

   _____

2. How are you leading others through places of danger, providing them with protection and instruction on how to live in the midst of those realities?

   _____

   _____

   _____

3. How are you leading others to a life in the kingdom of God?

_____

_____

_____

Pray for the countries of south Asia today. The countries in this area of the world are Bangladesh, Bhutan, India, Maldives, Nepal, Pakistan, and Sri Lanka. Though the land area of this region is relatively small, it is home for about a third of the world's population. The major religions are Hinduism, Buddhism, and Islam. Praise God for the missionary movement in India. Most workers are from the south of the country and are trying to spread the gospel in the difficult regions to the north. Extreme poverty and even slavery exist in some of these countries. Pray that freedom in Christ would advance throughout the region. Pray also that there would be more openness to the kingdom of God in all of these countries.

Notes

When We Are Overwhelmed

Jesus replied, "Now you believe? Look! A time is coming—and is here!
—when each of you will be scattered to your own homes and you will leave
me alone. I'm not really alone, for the Father is with me. I've said these
things to you so that you will have peace in me. In the world you have
distress. But be encouraged! I have conquered the world."

JOHN 16:31-33

*W*e have all experienced the feeling of being overwhelmed! For ou, perhaps the feeling is caused by being buried under too many things on your to-do list each day, or maybe from being so far under a mountain of school debt that, if there is light at the end of the tunnel, you may not live to see it!

Feeling overwhelmed is something that all people experience, in all levels of society and in all cultures. Of course, the things that overwhelm you or me might be considered a blessing by someone else. As university students face finals and term papers they may feel overwhelmed, while most people around the world would feel blessed to have such things in their lives. The underwater feeling, though, is a personal one—one that should not be compared to another person's existence. What we are experiencing is real for us, and that is what matters to us at that moment.

Cross-cultural mission workers do not get a pass when it comes to feeling overwhelmed. If anything, living cross-culturally adds to the possibility. Can you imagine dealing with what you must deal with daily, and then adding the cross-cultural element? That can mean operating in a different language, not understanding the verbal and nonverbal clues around you because they are based in a different cultural history, and possibly looking different from everyone else so that you feel like you truly live in a fishbowl. Living cross-culturally can be a life of stress on steroids.

Since we all deal with it, what do we do about it?

Here are some ideas to consider.

Breath in and breathe out. Remember that you are not alone. We all deal with the stress of being overwhelmed by one thing or another. Share your feelings with someone who loves you. "A three-ply cord doesn't easily snap" (Ecclesiastes 4:12).

Breathe in and breathe out. Rest in and meditate on God, knowing that he knows you fully and cares for you. "Only in God do I find rest; my salvation comes from him" (Psalm 62:1).

WHEN WE are OVERWHELMED

Breathe in and breathe out. Ask for help. Sometimes we feel overwhelmed because we will not allow ourselves to ask others to bear the weight with us. "Where two or three are gathered in my name, I'm there with them" (Matthew 18:20).

Breathe in and breathe out. Declutter. Begin by listing everything you have on your plate. How much of that list needs to be there? Sometimes you must let go of good things because you have taken on too many of them. Too many good things can be a bad thing! "What does the Lord require of you but to do justice, and to love kindness, and to walk humbly with your God?" (Micah 6:8 ESV).

Breathe in and breathe out. Seek professional help. If after sharing with a friend, things still seem out of control, ask for help from a professional. Financial planners, counselors, and organizational specialists, among others, may be able to help you get back into balance. "Plans fail with no counsel, but with many counselors they succeed" (Proverbs 15:22).

Whether you are in your home culture or in a different culture, remember that Jesus told us this world would include difficulty, but then he said,

"Be encouraged! I have conquered the world."

Questions for Reflection

1. What things are making you feel overwhelmed or out of control?

2. Who in your network would you trust to share these pressures with, both for emotional support and to help you carry the load?

3. Do you know of a counselor who may be able to help you when needed? If not, maybe you should ask some trusted friends who they would recommend.

_____

_____

_____

— *Pray for the Kingdom* —

Today, pray for the countries of east Asia. These countries include China, Japan, North Korea, South Korea, Mongolia, eastern Russia, and Taiwan. This region of the world is vast and also boasts about a third of the world's population. North Korea is one of the most difficult places for kingdom workers, and yet South Korea ranks only behind the United States in the number of missionaries sent out. Since the fall of the Soviet Union, there has been a rebirth of the growth of the church in the Russian Federation, but these areas, such as Siberia, are difficult to live in. Praise God for the growth of the church in Mongolia. They are now hoping to send missionaries everywhere the Mongol Empire once existed!

— *Notes* —

DAY TWENTY FOUR

Only Some of Us Will Listen

Then I heard the Lord's voice saying,
"Whom should I send, and who will go for us?"
I said, "I'm here; send me."
God said, "Go ..."
ISAIAH 6:8-9A

*T*ruth can be spoken to us from some of the most interesting places. One of those places is the movie *The Santa Clause.* In the movie Scott Calvin, played by Tim Allen, finds himself at the North Pole with his young son. As he looks around, he comments to an elf that he can't believe what he is seeing. The elf responds, "Seeing isn't believing. Believing is seeing."

That is a pretty good definition of faith, coming from the script of a family Christmas movie. That statement has been there since the screenplay was written, but few consider its underlying meaning:

Only some of us will listen.

In his book *The Gifts of the Jews,* Thomas Cahill proposes that God possibly spoke to many people in the Sumerian culture of Ur. What made Abram different was that he listened—and obeyed. Cahill says one of the most pivotal statements in history is, "So, Abram went, as the Lord had told him." Abram not only listened to what God was telling him; he obeyed, and the world was changed forever.

Could it be that God is speaking to many of us who call ourselves Christ-followers, asking us to engage our communities, or the communities he will send us to, for the kingdom, but that *only some of us will listen*? I do not want to lay a guilt trip on you. I am, though, asking if you are taking time to hear from God about how he wants you to be involved in his work. The needs are staggering both here and around the world. All you have to do is respond in obedience to what God is asking you to do about it.

Are you listening?

If you haven't really been paying attention and you think your opportunity has passed you by, don't worry. You won't miss it. Jesus tells us that his people hear and know his voice, like sheep can discern the voice of their shepherd from the other voices around them. Clearly, hearing his voice will require slowing down and taking time to listen. We are all so busy, but Jesus is patient and persistent. If he is able to influence the decisions of biblical people like Pharaoh and Nebuchadnezzar, he is certainly able to direct you and me, as we are listening for his voice.

Will you go?

Abram did, and God built on that obedience to bless us, and the whole world, through him in Jesus. Moses did, though not without a bit of complaining, and he was considered the friend of God. David did, and he was considered a man after God's own heart. Paul did, and the gospel was brought to the non-Jew (that is, most of us!). Jesus did, and as a result we have the opportunity to be called the children of God and to be joint heirs with Christ to the kingdom of God.

Questions for Reflection

1. How do you listen for God's voice? When you read the Bible are you reading to hear something?

   _____

   _____

   _____

2. Sometimes God wants to speak to us when we are praying. When you pray, who does most of the talking?

   _____

   _____

   _____

3. When God does speak to you, are you ready to obey? Have you already committed to follow him no matter what the cost?

   _____

   _____

   _____

Pray for the Kingdom

Pray for the countries of southeast Asia today, including Brunei, Cambodia, Indonesia, Laos, Malaysia, Myanmar, Philippines, Singapore, Thailand, East Timor, and Vietnam. The major religions in these countries are Islam, Buddhism, animism, and Christianity. Singapore and the Philippines are the biggest missionary sending countries in the region. Pray that God will continue to call many from those countries to take his message elsewhere. The church is growing, though slowly, in Myanmar, Cambodia, Laos, and East Timor. Pray for more openness in Brunei, Indonesia, Malaysia, Thailand, and Vietnam. Also pray for the disciple-making movements that are sweeping this area, that more leaders would be identified and that decisions to follow Christ would take hold and flourish.

Notes

Leave a Legacy

Love the Lord your God with all your heart, all your being, and all your strength. These words that I am commanding you today must always be on your minds. Recite them to your children. Talk about them when you are sitting around your house and when you are out and about, when you are lying down and when you are getting up. Tie them on your hand as a sign. They should be on your forehead as a symbol. Write them on your house's doorframes and on your city's gates.

DEUTERONOMY 6:5-9

*M*ost of us probably don't put much thought toward our legacy because we think it is something that you put off until you're older. Nothing could be farther from the truth. The truth is that you are creating your legacy every moment you are alive.

The decisions you make today shape the world you will live in tomorrow, for you and the others around you. The way you live out each moment will impact your future, your children's future, and your grandchildren's future, should you be blessed to have them.

Be intentional. Be proactive.

Here are some simple ways to live out your legacy today:

Be known as someone who prays. Our greatest impact on the world around us comes through prayer. Make it a habit. Live each moment as an expression of prayer (see 1 Thessalonians 5:17).

Be known as someone who faces life with joy. Joy is more than happiness. Joy is contentment that results from knowing that there is a deeper truth than the circumstances that sway us. It is realizing that, of all the possible paths we could take, we are on the right one (see 1 Thessalonians 5:16).

Be known as someone who is thankful. Thank those who serve you, even though it may be their job to do so. Thank your family for how they love you. Thank your friends for how they stand by you, even when you are wrong (see 1 Thessalonians 5:18).

Be known as someone who is loyal. Jesus sacrificed himself for us. Pursue that kind of commitment for those around you (see Philippians 2:5-8).

Be known as someone who puts others first. Our culture today is overrun with selfishness. The "me generation" is every generation. Stand against the current (see Philippians 2:4).

Be known as someone who seeks and lives for the kingdom. This is not easy to do, but the Bible gives us a guide. Live a life that demonstrates the fruit of the Spirit. Make the kingdom a priority and everything else will fall into place (see Matthew 6:33).

Be known as someone who loves others. "Love bears all things, believes all things, hopes all things, endures all things. Love never ends" (1 Corinthians 13:7-8a ESV).

A legacy must be created in community. Hermits don't leave a legacy, because their lives are not lived out interacting with others. Your world will change as you engage it for change.

Make a difference that lasts.

Start today. Start now.

Questions for Reflection

1. Have you committed the fruit of the Spirit to memory? You might try that now: love, joy, peace, patience, kindness, goodness, faithfulness, gentleness, and self-control.

2. What would it look like in your life to put others first? How would you need to change the way you live, the way you see life?

3. How often do you genuinely thank the people around you?

Pray for The Kingdom

Today, pray for the countries of north Africa. Those countries are Algeria, Chad, Egypt, Libya, Mali, Mauritania, Morocco, Tunisia, Western Sahara, Niger, and Sudan. All are predominantly Islamic countries. Egypt has an Orthodox strain of Christianity called the Coptic church. You may remember the story of many Coptics being killed recently by militant, Islamic radicals. Pray that believers in these countries would have the depth of faith necessary to hold on to what they believe in the face of this kind of persecution. Pray for the missionaries who work in northern Africa. Many of them are from Latin American countries and are not treated well. Pray for more kingdom workers and more financial resources to be focused on this part of the world.

Notes

Improvising the Gospel

The apostles and the brothers and sisters throughout Judea heard
that even the Gentiles had welcomed God's word. When Peter went up
to Jerusalem, the circumcised believers criticized him. They accused him,
"You went into the home of the uncircumcised and ate with them!" Step-by-step,
Peter explained what had happened.... Once the apostles and other believers
heard this, they calmed down. They praised God and concluded,
"So then God has enabled Gentiles to change their hearts
and lives so that they might have new life."

ACTS 11:1-4, 18

*A*re you a fan of jazz? Some people are, and some aren't. Those of us who are understand a little about improvising on a theme. Often the theme is a well-known older song, called a standard, but sometimes the theme is just a melody line that is created in the moment by one of the musicians. Whether from a standard or from a creative moment, the theme is introduced by one of the players. Then another player picks up the theme and improvises on it, adding their own stylings and creation to the theme while keeping the theme present.

In the cross-cultural mission world, we improvise on the gospel all the time. We take the gospel and contextualize it to the culture we are working in. Language is often the first area where we feel this need. Perhaps you are in a culture that has never experienced snow. If you were teaching from Isaiah 1:18, which talks about God taking our scarlet sin and making it white as snow, you would need to come up with another way to explain what that Scripture meant. You wouldn't change the message of the verse, but the people wouldn't understand it well unless you changed the metaphor. Bible translators are constantly faced with this challenge.

Differences in cultures make improvising necessary as well. For example, tribal cultures tend to see God as a chief and relate him to what they have experienced through the ages from human chiefs. Mission workers must find ways to help them understand an all-powerful yet loving God that make sense to them. Cultures who have endured centuries of being dominated by another culture struggle with understanding true freedom in Christ. In the U.S., we are so individualistic we make our faith out to be very personal, when that may not be the emphasis of much of Scripture. We could go on and on here with current examples, but the Bible addresses this as well.

When Paul is talking with the Athenians on Mars Hill he begins by relating to their own spirituality, knowing that they worship many gods faithfully. He goes on to say that they even have a monument for an unknown god, wanting to make sure they cover all their bases. He then tells them about God, but in that discussion quotes from their own philosophers to illustrate his points. Paul writes about his way of improvising on the gospel in 1 Corinthians 9:19-22:

Although I'm free from all people, I make myself a slave to all people,
to recruit more of them.... I act like I'm under the Law to those under the Law,
so I can recruit those who are under the Law (though I myself am not under the
Law). I act like I'm outside the Law to those who are outside the Law, so I can
recruit those outside the Law (though I'm not outside the law of God but
rather under the law of Christ). I act weak to the weak, so I can recruit
the weak. I have become all things to all people, so
I could save some by all possible means.

How should this impact your life today living in your home culture?

In your improvisation of the gospel, remember to remain true to the theme. Let the gospel always be present and clear although you have personalized it and contextualized it. It is the power of God leading to salvation for all who believe.

Questions for Reflection

1. Can you see how improvising on the themes of Scripture is important to making the message of the gospel clear to other cultures?

   _____

   _____

   _____

2. How might you improvise the message through your life to impact those around you?

   _____

   _____

   _____

3. What would be an example of when an improvisation goes too far?

   _____

   _____

   _____

— *Pray for the Kingdom* —

Today, pray for the countries of western and central Africa. These countries include Benin, Burkina Faso, Cameroon, Cape Verde, Central African Republic, Djibouti, Eritrea, Ethiopia, Gambia, Ghana, Guinea, Guinea Bissau, Côte d'Ivoire, Liberia, Nigeria, Senegal, Sierra Leone, Somalia, South Sudan, and Togo. The countries in this part of Africa fall into three general categories with somewhat similar needs in each category. The countries with a majority of Christ-followers (Benin, Cameroon, Cape Verde, Central African Republic, Ghana, Liberia, and Togo) need prayer for more leadership development, pastor training, discipleship, and unity. The countries where Islam is the majority religion (Burkina Faso, Djibouti, Gambia, Guinea, Guinea Bissau, Senegal, Sierra Leone, and Somalia) need prayer for more widespread evangelism in the face of significant persecution, church growth and multiplication, openness to the gospel, peace in some countries, and open doors for ministry. The third grouping of countries would be those in which the percentage of Christ-followers and Muslims is about the same (Eritrea, Ethiopia, Côte d'Ivoire, Nigeria, and South Sudan). The greatest prayer requests in these countries are for peace, religious freedom, church health and growth, discipleship, and missionary sending.

— *Notes* —

Set the World on Fire

*Christ is just like the human body—a body is a unit and has
many parts; and all the parts of the body are one body, even though there
are many. We were all baptized by one Spirit into one body, whether Jew
or Greek, or slave or free, and we all were given one Spirit to drink.*
1 CORINTHIANS 12:12-13

*C*atherine of Siena was a Dominican tertiary (a tertiary is a layperson considered part of a monastic order) in the 1300s, but her words still hold a great challenge for us today:

"Be who God meant you to be and you will set the world on fire."

She lived this statement, refusing to marry as her parents wished, and committing herself completely to the service of God and of others. Catherine had tremendous impact on her world for two major reasons:

- She had a clear vision (leading) from God.
- She obeyed that leading and stuck to it when things got tough.

She also said,

"Nothing great is ever achieved without much enduring."

Most of us want to live lives of significance. We want our lives to count for the kingdom and hear God say "Well done" when we finally stand before him. Sometimes we are fooled into thinking that we must do something great, something notorious, to make that kind of impact. We look at our Christian "idols" and say, "If only I could write a song like that" or "If only I could preach like that, then I could really make a difference." The truth is that we can all make a difference with the opportunities God provides us if we are just willing to make use of them for God's glory.

One other thing we need to remember as we get out there to change the world is that we can only be who God created us to be. The apostle Paul reminds us that the church is like the body of Christ. Each of us has different parts to play within the body—some flashy and some not so flashy—but all equally critical to the healthy functioning of the body. When we try to play a part we were not meant to play, we appear inauthentic, as if we are forcing something.

No matter what your passion, gifting, experience, or education, pursue obedience with all that you are and keep at it, even when the road gets difficult. Remember Catherine's words, "Nothing great is ever achieved without much enduring." Don't waste time looking at what others are doing or comparing "results" with someone else. Nothing of value ever comes from that. As Jesus told Peter when he tried to compare his future with the apostle John's, "What is it to you if I want him to live until I return? You must follow me" (John 21:22 CEV).

You be you. Let God be God, and let him worry about all the rest. He is the one with the power to bring about his will, and he will ultimately get all the glory. Let's walk the path God has laid out for us and do so with passion and endurance.

That is how we will set the world on fire!

Questions for Reflection

1. What passions do you have in your life? How have you gone about pursuing them?

   _____

   _____

   _____

2. Have there been things that you thought you could, or should, try but have felt you could not succeed?

   _____

   _____

   _____

3. Have you ever thought of asking for help from others in the family of God to achieve something that seems beyond you?

   _____

   _____

   _____

— Pray for the Kingdom —

Today pray for the countries of southern Africa: Angola, Botswana, Burundi, Comoros, Democratic Republic of Congo, Republic of Congo, Equatorial Guinea, Eswatini, Gabon, Kenya, Lesotho, Madagascar, Mauritius, Mozambique, Namibia, Rwanda, São Tomé and Príncipe, Seychelles, South Africa, Swaziland, Tanzania, Uganda, Zambia, and Zimbabwe. Christianity is the majority religion in nearly all the countries in Africa's southern cone. Pray for revival as nominalism and Christianity as tradition are evident everywhere. Pray for growth in leadership training, especially in the rural areas of most countries. Finally, pray for the growing missions movement from this area to the least-reached countries of North Africa. The countries that are not predominately Christian are Comoros, where just 1 percent of the population would identify as Christian, Madagascar and Mozambique, where the church is growing but a large percentage of people are still animistic, and Mauritius, where the majority religion is Hindu, although over 30 percent of the population identify as Christian. Pray for evangelistic efforts in these countries. Pray for courage for Christ-followers in the face of persecution. Pray for peace and recovery, as many of these countries have been in conflict both externally and internally.

— Notes —

Just Show Up

I was circumcised on the eighth day.
I am from the people of Israel and the tribe of Benjamin.
I am a Hebrew of the Hebrews.
With respect to observing the Law, I'm a Pharisee.
With respect to devotion to the faith, I harassed the church.
With respect to righteousness under the Law, I'm blameless.
These things were my assets, but I wrote them off as a loss for the sake
of Christ. But even beyond that, I consider everything a loss in comparison
with the superior value of knowing Christ Jesus my Lord. I have lost
everything for him, but what I lost I think of as sewer trash,
so that I might gain Christ and be found in him.
PHILIPPIANS 3:5-9A

**If we have kingdom impact, it will be because
we have made ourselves available to the King.**

As we considered in the last reflection, we often think we must do something great for God when all that is really needed is that we just show up. The more we try to control each day, the less we are submissive to the Spirit's control. The more we rely on our own power and ability, the less open we are to be used to display God's power.

It's possible that some of these thoughts come from the stories of the Bible. We seem to remember the stories that have bigger-than-life heroes in them, like Abraham, Moses, David, Peter, and Paul. We need to remember that there were many other people serving God who are not mentioned. They went about their daily lives in selfless obedience and brought glory to God that way. Maybe you remember the story of Naaman, a general in the Syrian army. When he got leprosy and was out of options it was a little slave girl who suggested he go see Elisha the prophet. He did and was healed and became a God-follower. He was a person of great power, and yet an unnamed child of God saved his life.

The apostle Paul was a pretty powerful guy too, and yet he writes to the church in Philippi that he considers his heritage, gifting, and training to be "loss for the sake of Christ" (Philippians 3:7b ESV). He counted all his ability as "garbage." In his second letter to the church in Corinth he says that he will boast in his weakness because it is in our weakness that God's perfect strength is shown (2 Corinthians 12:9 my paraphrase). How often are we willing to allow ourselves to be weak?

What are you depending on to make your mark on history? Sometimes the things we think are going to be our greatest advantage actually hold us back from what God can accomplish in and through us.

Lay it on the altar.

The children of Israel were facing the Red Sea. The Egyptians were bearing down on them. They had nowhere to go and no resources to defend themselves. Moses' words to them were clear and should ring out to us today: "Stand still and see the salvation of the Lord." (Exodus 14:13 KJV) We know the rest of the story. God parts the sea. The Israelites walk through to the other side. The army of Egypt follows and is destroyed as the sea returns to normal.

Hope comes from hopelessness.

Strength comes in weakness.

Peace is found amid the storm.

Want to impact the world for the kingdom?

Just show up!

Questions for Reflection

1. In what areas of your life are you afraid to be weak?

   _____

   _____

2. In what areas of your life to you feel strong and confident?

   _____

   _____

3. Do you have potential opportunities to minister but are avoiding them because you are not confident? Do you tend to do the things you are confident about without spending much time before the Lord?

   _____

   _____

Pray for the Kingdom

Today pray for the countries of Oceania. These countries are Australia, Federated States of Micronesia, Fiji, Kiribati, Marshall Islands, Nauru, New Zealand, Palau, Papua New Guinea, Samoa, Solomon Islands, Tonga, Tuvalu, and Vanuatu. With the exceptions of Australia, Fiji, and New Zealand, all the island countries in this region are over 96 percent Christian. The other three are majority Christian but at lower percentages. Fiji has a large percentage of Hindus, and Australia and New Zealand have large percentages of nonreligious people. Pray against nominalism in these countries and for strong church leadership. Pray also for the missions movement from many of these countries. Leadership development continues to be a need as well as unity among believers.

Notes

Missing the Miracle

When he came to his hometown, he taught the people in their synagogue.
They were surprised and said, "Where did he get this wisdom? Where did
he get the power to work miracles? Isn't he the carpenter's son? Isn't his
mother named Mary? Aren't James, Joseph, Simon, and Judas his
brothers? And his sisters, aren't they here with us? Where did this
man get all this?" They were repulsed by him and fell into sin.

But Jesus said to them, "Prophets are honored everywhere except
in their own hometowns and in their own households." He was
unable to do many miracles there because of their disbelief.

MATTHEW 13:54-58

*N*ext to them the people from Tekoa made repairs, but their officials wouldn't help with the work of their supervisors" (Nehemiah 3:5). Nehemiah 3 is one of those Scripture passages that most of us pass by, because it just lists who worked on what section of the walls of Jerusalem during the rebuilding organized by Nehemiah. There is something for us kingdom workers, though, in this verse.

Though the men of Tekoa repaired their part— and even repaired an additional section of the wall, going above and beyond the call to work— their nobles did not. We don't know why they chose to sit out, but we could all make guesses. Their reasoning doesn't really matter. What matters is what we read a few chapters later in Nehemiah 6:15-16:

So the wall was finished on the twenty-fifth day of the month of Elul. It took fifty-two days. When our enemies heard about this, all of the nations around us were afraid and their confidence was greatly shaken. They knew that this work was completed with the help of our God.

Fifty-two days! That would be a tremendous feat even if a modern construction company were involved. In fact, it would be impossible for a construction company to complete a wall of that size in fifty-two days! The people who completed this task were priests and goldsmiths and other regular people. One dad even had his daughters out there. The whole community came together, and God used them to bring about the impossible. The whole community except the nobles of Tekoa, that is. They took themselves out of the game and missed being part of the miracle.

Don't miss out on the miracles God has planned for you.

Engage! Be part of what God is doing here and around the world. The reality is that we never know when God is going to get involved and bring about the impossible. We just need to be faithful to respond in obedience to what he asks of us, bring our needs to him in prayer, and apply ourselves with all that we are. If you can, be like the people of Tekoa and take on a double portion! When God brings about impossible things you will have been part of it.

One more thing should be said here. To see God do the impossible in and through us, we must make ourselves available for things that are beyond what is possible. I am sure none of the people in Nehemiah's time thought what they accomplished would be possible in fifty-two days, but they put themselves to the task anyway. You'll never know if you can walk on water until you get out of the boat!

Questions for Reflection

1. Are there things needed in your life that seem impossible?

    _____

    _____

    _____

2. Is being overwhelmed by the task ahead keeping you from taking action?

    _____

    _____

    _____

3. How would seeing God do the impossible change the way you live life?

    _____

    _____

    _____

Pray for the Kingdom

Pray for the peoples of the Islamic faith today. Of the three major non-Christian religions, Islam is the most like what we believe. God is moving in miraculous ways in the lives of Muslims. He is appearing to them in dreams and telling them to seek out Christ-followers. The conflict between Islamic sects has created many refugees and this has pushed many to seek a different faith. Discipleship Making Movements (DMMs) are an effective ministry in Islamic countries. The result of all this is that tens of thousands of Muslims are beginning to follow Jesus. Even with all this positive news it is still true that more than 80 percent of Muslims don't even know a Christ-follower. Much work is yet to be done. Pray for more workers in that harvest field!

Notes

I Am Willing

Large crowds followed Jesus as he came down the mountainside.
Suddenly, a man with leprosy approached him and knelt before him. "Lord,"
the man said, "if you are willing, you can heal me and make me clean."

Jesus reached out and touched him. "I am willing," he said. "Be healed!"
And instantly the leprosy disappeared. Then Jesus said to him, "Don't tell
anyone about this. Instead, go to the priest and let him examine you. Take
along the offering required in the law of Moses for those who have been healed
of leprosy. This will be a public testimony that you have been cleansed.". .

MATTHEW 8:1-4 NLT

*T*here was little reason to hope. He had heard rumors of this Jesus who could heal the sick; but what were his chances? Little to none. He was a leper, an outcast, banned from being near anyone. Certainly, Jesus was always surrounded by people needing him, wanting him. How would he get close enough?

News came into the area that Jesus was close by. Some fishermen who let him use their boat from which to speak had then pulled in a record number of fish. Now was his chance. He would try to see Jesus. What did he have to lose?

He found a place close enough to the road, but still out of sight, from which to make his desperate approach. As Jesus walked by, he made his move, pushing through the crowd and causing a huge commotion, to fall before this healer.

Jesus stopped and looked at him. Words tumbled out. "Lord, if you are willing, you can heal me and make me clean." Jesus reached out and touched him. "I am willing," he said smiling, "Be healed!" Immediately the leprosy was gone!

This leper represents each of us. Our need is beyond what we can handle. Our hopelessness is clear. His willingness is our redemption and salvation. He is our healing. He is our wholeness, our completeness, and our only hope. Many times, we think of this story in regard to salvation, which is appropriate, but that isn't the only time we are in need of Jesus' willingness. As sheep of the Good Shepherd we are in constant need of his direction, protection, and provision. If we are honest with ourselves, we need his willingness every hour of every day!

"I am willing. Be healed!"

What can we possibly do in response to such an action of love, forgiveness, grace, and hope?

At the same time the church was being born within the Jewish community, there were also those outside that culture who were responding to the grace of God. Cornelius was one of those people, a centurion in the Italian Regiment. God told him in a vision to send for Peter. Peter had a vision as well, in which God showed him that all things he had created were clean and valuable to him. Just then the messengers from Cornelius arrived. Peter went with them, and all Cornelius's household was brought into the kingdom as a result.

Visiting a Gentile in their home was forbidden to the Jews. Peter, though, in response to God's love for him through Jesus, was willing to obey God's direction, and that obedience helped change the course of the church. We are part of the family of God today in part because of Peter's "I am willing" response.

Whatever God is asking of you today, will you be willing to respond?

"I am willing."

Questions for Reflection

1. Do you feel that God is prompting you to get involved in something new?

2. Have you been willing, or have you hesitated for one reason or another?

3. What roadblocks are keeping you from being completely open to pursuing what God is leading you toward?

Pray for the Kingdom

Pray for the people of the Hindu faith today. Hinduism is the third-largest religion by population, with more than one billion adherents, and is predominant in India, Nepal, and Mauritius as well as in Bali, Indonesia. Hindus are tolerant of many faiths, and even their own faith has many different sects. Some believe in one supreme deity while others hold to thirty-three or more deities. Hindus do not tend to be tolerant of Christianity, though, as many believers are persecuted heavily. Pray that God, through his Holy Spirit's work, will break through to the people of the Hindu faith. Pray for more harvesters who are willing to engage the people of this religion even in the face of possible difficultly. Pray for the hundreds of Indian missionaries already taking the good news to their Hindu neighbors!

Notes

Armed with a Peashooter

Thanks be to God, who gives us this victory through our Lord Jesus Christ! As a result of all this, my loved brothers and sisters, you must stand firm, unshakable, excelling in the work of the Lord as always, because you know that your labor isn't going to be for nothing in the Lord.

1 CORINTHIANS 15:57-58

*O*ur spiritual enemy has an impressive arsenal of weaponry at his disposal to use against us and yet, way too often, we choose a peashooter with which to enter the battle. For some reason we convince ourselves that our natural resources will win the day against supernatural forces. Though that may make a best-selling movie script, it is not, in fact, reality.

The reality is that we are hopelessly lost in this warfare without relying on God's armor and arsenal. The apostle Paul tells us in Ephesians 6:12 what is really going on around us:

We aren't fighting against human enemies
but against rulers, authorities, forces of cosmic darkness,
and spiritual powers of evil in the heavens.

Our situation looks grim, but read on.

So stand with the belt of truth around your waist, justice
as your breastplate, and put shoes on your feet so that you are
ready to spread the good news of peace. Above all, carry the shield
of faith so that you can extinguish the flaming arrows of the
evil one. Take the helmet of salvation. (verses 14-17)

God has given us a great defense in his truth, his righteousness, his gospel, his faith, and his salvation, but that's not all. We can go on the offensive with weapons that the enemy knows will defeat him.

And the sword of the Spirit, which is God's word.
Offer prayers and petitions in the Spirit all the time. Stay alert
by hanging in there and praying for all believers. (verses 17-18)

The "word of God," both written (the Bible) and living (Jesus), will bring us to God's victory. How do we wield it?

Prayer.

Prayer seems like such a simple thing, but in the end, it is the most powerful thing. Prayer brings to bear the power of God. As in most things spiritual, reality is upside down. What we perceive as weak is strong. What appears to be loss is gain. Satan's greatest victory, in crucifying the Christ, is his ultimate defeat. Praise be to God!

Make a renewed commitment to do battle in prayer, making use of our greatest spiritual resource!

Questions for Reflection

1. Do you often feel that you come to prayer as a last resort when things are not working well?

    _____

    _____

    _____

2. How do you view the power of prayer, and how does that affect how you use it?

    _____

    _____

    _____

3. What steps can you take to make prayer a more consistent first line of action in your life?

    _____

    _____

    _____

Pray for the Kingdom

Pray for people of the Buddhist faith today. Buddhism is a state religion in six countries in Asia and has significant influence in ten other countries. The fall of communism in many countries has encouraged a growth in adherents to Buddhism and the popularity of the Dalai Lama of Tibet has influenced growth in the religion in the West. Evangelism in countries committed to Buddhism is extremely difficult, with low conversion rates. Pray for more missionaries willing to engage Buddhists, for their prayer and financial support, and for encouragement. Pray that the Holy Spirit would break through the spiritual strongholds of this religion, that there would be an openness to consider the claims of Christ.

Notes

Made in USA - Kendallville, IN
1048502_9781702769204
02 05 2020 0808